Budge TROLL, Budge!

Level 5D

Written by Louise Goodman
Illustrated by Nicola Anderson

What is synthetic phonics?

Synthetic phonics teaches children to recognise the sounds of letters and to blend (synthesise) them together to make whole words.

Understanding sound/letter relationships gives children the confidence and ability to read unfamiliar words, without having to rely on memory or guesswork; this helps them to progress towards independent reading.

Did you know? Spoken English uses more than 40 speech sounds. Each sound is called a *phoneme*. Some phonemes relate to a single letter (d-o-g) and others to combinations of letters (sh-ar-p). When a phoneme is written down it is called a *grapheme*. Teaching these sounds, matching them to their written form and sounding out words for reading is the basis of synthetic phonics.

Consultant

I love reading phonics has been created in consultation with language expert Abigail Steel. She has a background in teaching and teacher training and is a respected expert in the field of synthetic phonics. Abigail Steel is a regular contributor to educational publications. Her international education consultancy supports parents and teachers in the promotion of literacy skills.

Reading tips

This book focuses on the j sound, made with the letters ge and dge: j as in barge and hedge.

Tricky words in this book

Any words in bold may have unusual spellings or are new and have not yet been introduced.

> Tricky words in this book:
>
> **would**

Extra ways to have fun with this book

After the reader has read the story, ask them questions about what they have just read:

Can you remember some words that contain the different sounds shown by the letter j?
Which character in the book was your favourite, and why?

Don't even think about eating me, I'm having a bad enough day already!

A pronunciation guide

This grid contains the sounds used in the stories in levels 4, 5 and 6 and a guide on how to say them. /**a**/ represents the sounds made, rather than the letters in a word.

/**ai**/ as in game	/**ai**/ as in play/they	/**ee**/ as in leaf/these	/**ee**/ as in he
/**igh**/ as in kite/light	/**igh**/ as in find/sky	/**oa**/ as in home	/**oa**/ as in snow
/**oa**/ as in cold	/**y+oo**/ as in cube/music/new	long /**oo**/ as in flute/crew/blue	/**oi**/ as in boy
/**er**/ as in bird/hurt	/**or**/ as in snore/oar/door	/**or**/ as in dawn/sauce/walk	/**e**/ as in head
/**e**/ as in said/any	/**ou**/ as in cow	/**u**/ as in touch	/**air**/ as in hare/bear/there
/**eer**/ as in deer/here/cashier	/**t**/ as in tripped/skipped	/**d**/ as in rained	/**j**/ as in gent/gin/gym
/**j**/ as in barge/hedge	/**s**/ as in cent/circus/cyst	/**s**/ as in prince	/**s**/ as in house
/**ch**/ as in itch/catch	/**w**/ as in white	/**h**/ as in who	/**r**/ as in write/rhino

Sounds this story focuses on are highlighted in the grid.

/**f**/ as in phone	/**f**/ as in rough	/**ul**/ as in pencil/ hospital	/**z**/ as in fries/ cheese/breeze
/**n**/ as in knot/ gnome/engine	/**m**/ as in welcome /thumb/column	/**g**/ as in guitar/ghost	/**zh**/ as in vision/beige
/**k**/ as in chord	/**k**/ as in plaque/ bouquet	/**nk**/ as in uncle	/**ks**/ as in box/books/ ducks/cakes
/**a**/ and /**o**/ as in hat/what	/**e**/ and /**ee**/ as in bed/he	/**i**/ and /**igh**/ as in fin/find	/**o**/ and /**oa**/ as in hot/cold
/**u**/ and short /**oo**/ as in but/put	/**ee**/, /**e**/ and /**ai**/ as in eat/ bread/break	/**igh**/, /**ee**/ and /**e**/ as in tie/field/friend	/**ou**/ and /**oa**/ as in cow/blow
/**ou**/, /**oa**/ and /**oo**/ as in out/ shoulder/could	/**i**/ and /**ai**/ as in money/they	/**c**/ and /**s**/ as in cat/cent	/**y**/, /**igh**/ and /**i**/ as in yes/sky/myth
/**g**/ and /**j**/ as in got/giant	/**ch**/, /**c**/ and /**sh**/ as in chin/ school/chef	/**er**/, /**air**/ and /**eer**/ as in earth/bear/ears	/**u**/, /**ou**/ and /**oa**/ as in plough/dough

Be careful not to add an 'uh' sound to 's', 't', 'p', 'c', 'h', 'r', 'm', 'd', 'g', 'l', 'f' and 'b'. For example, say 'fff' not 'fuh' and 'sss' not 'suh'.

Gerald the troll was large and
orange. He lived under the bridge.

When anyone tried to cross the bridge, he flew into a rage and **would** not budge.

One day a badger on a barge
came to the bridge.
"Let me pass! I'm on a trip."

"Stop right there!" said the troll.
"No badgers. I will not budge!"
And off he trudged.

Then a page boy, jumping over
a hedge, came to the bridge.
"Let me pass! I'm late for tea."

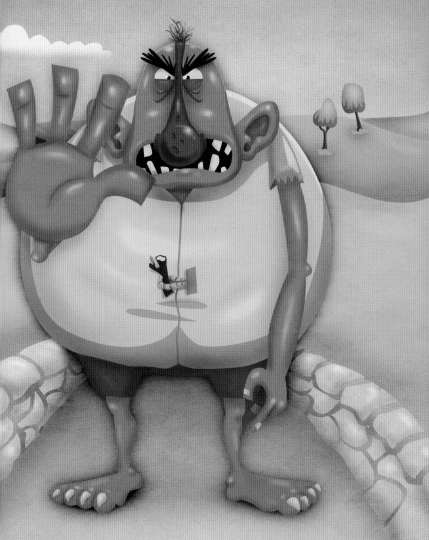

"Hold it!" said the troll. "No page boys." And off he trudged.

Next, a gingerbread man came
to the bridge.
"Let me pass! Have this fudge!"

"Out!" said the troll. "No gingerbread men!" And off he trudged.

Soon, a lady on a sledge came
to the bridge.
"Let me pass! Now!"

"Off with you!" said the troll.
"No ladies." And off he trudged.

Then one day, a judge came to the bridge. "Let me pass. That's an order!"

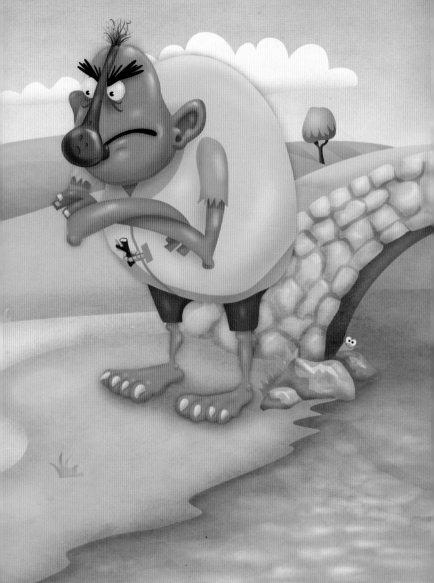

"Back off," said the troll. "I will not budge! Not even for a judge!" And off he trudged.

But then someone else came to the bridge. It was...

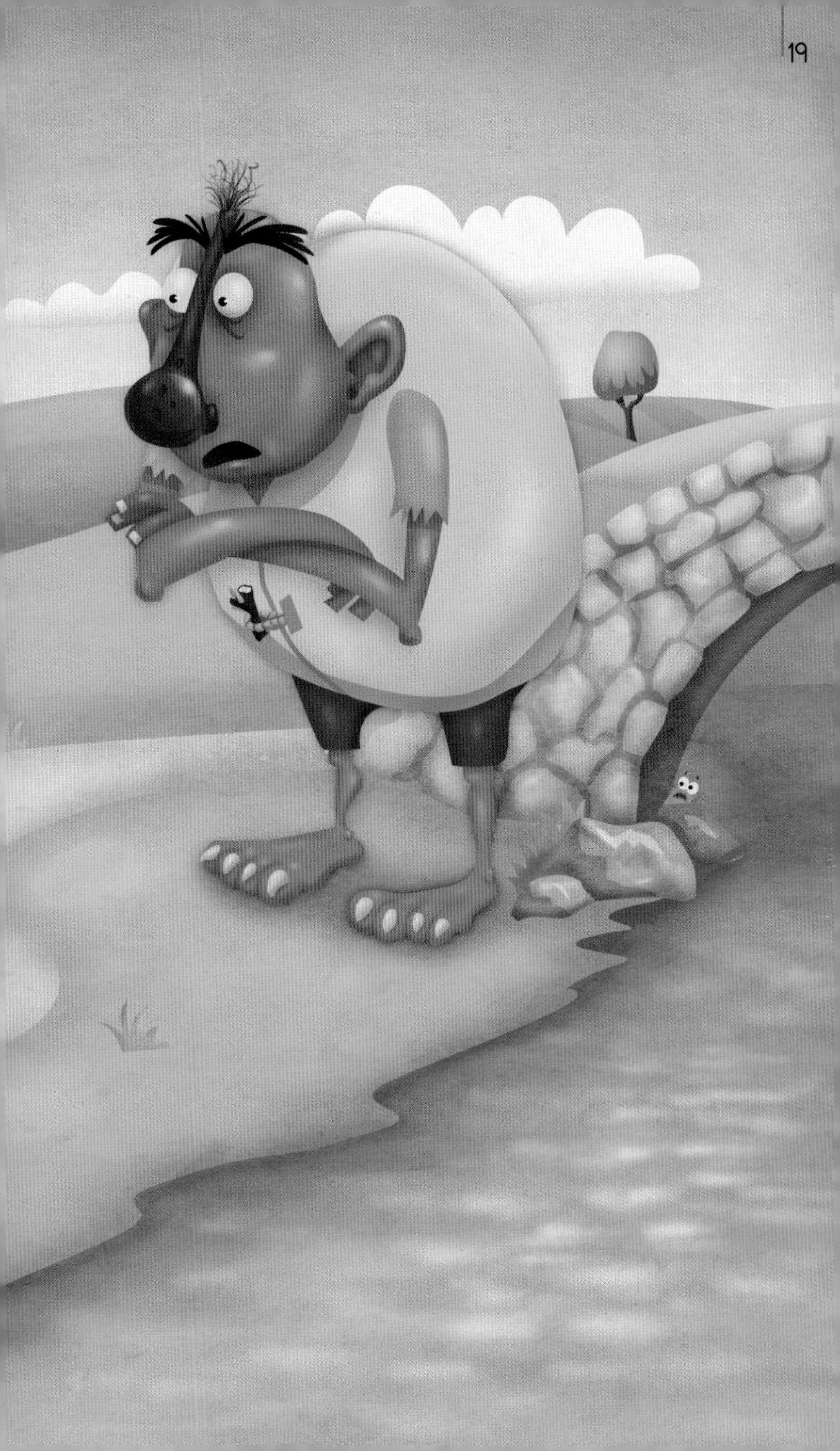

...another troll! He was orange...
He was in a rage... And he was
very, very large!

"Let me pass!" said the troll.

"Please do," said Gerald.

And off he trudged.

OVER 48 TITLES IN SIX LEVELS
Abigail Steel recommends...

Some titles from Level 4

I love reading phonics **The Maze**
978-1-84898-559-9

I love reading phonics **Fairy Fay's Bad Day**
978-1-84898-560-5

I love reading phonics **Pirate School**
978-1-84898-566-7

Other titles to enjoy from Level 5

I love reading phonics **Snapped by Sam**
978-1-84898-561-2

I love reading phonics **Max's Trip**
978-1-84898-562-9

I love reading phonics **George the Genius Gerbil**
978-1-84898-567-4

Some titles from Level 6

I love reading phonics **What Wally Wanted**
978-1-84898-563-6

I love reading phonics **Adine's Igloo**
978-1-84898-569-8

I love reading phonics **The Robot Bop**
978-1-84898-570-4

An Hachette UK Company
www.hachette.co.uk

Copyright © Octopus Publishing Group Ltd 2012
First published in Great Britain in 2012 by TickTock, an imprint of Octopus Publishing Group Ltd,
Endeavour House, 189 Shaftesbury Avenue, London WC2H 8JY.
www.octopusbooks.co.uk

ISBN 978 1 84898 568 1

Printed and bound in China
10 9 8 7 6 5 4 3 2 1